No Straight Lines

Robyn Black
No Straight Lines

Acknowledgements

'Bounced': published in *Regime (Books) Magazine* #3 2013

'Corey': Winner of the Joseph Furphy Commemorative Literary Award – Open Poetry 2009

'Raptor': Winner of the Joseph Furphy Commemorative Literary Award – Open Poetry 2010

'Boat Talk': Long-listed and published in the Long-list Anthology – inaugural Montreal International Poetry Prize 2011

'Bunyip': published on the Australia Poetry website

'Hand-knitting Peace', 'Rainbow Harmony', 'The Forming of Birds' and 'Transformed' were all written in collaboration with the Splinter Contemporary Artists (Goulburn Valley, Victoria) at the Shepparton Festival's Converge in 2019. The poetry and artworks were subsequently exhibited at Sharing Stories – Kyabram Town Hall in May 2019 and at the G.R.A.I.N. Store (Nathalia) Collaborative Art Exhibition November 2019.

A number of other poems have been published in various editions of *Tamba* (Goulburn Valley Writers Group Inc.)

No Straight Lines
ISBN 978 1 76109 177 3
Copyright © text Robyn Black 2021
Copyright © cover artwork Creagh Manning 2021

First published 2021 by
GINNINDERRA PRESS
PO Box 3461 Port Adelaide 5015 Australia
www.ginninderrapress.com.au

Contents

The Forming of Birds	7
Hand-knitting Peace	8
Rainbow Harmony	9
Transformed	10
Serpent's Tale	11
Story	12
Corey	14
Bunyip	16
Body Singing	17
Singing With Both Hands	18
Boat Talk	19
Amal's Voice	20
Aleppo	22
Syria	23
Yet Still We War	24
The Drowning of Angels	26
Unravelling	27
The Leaving of Angels	28
Arranging the Day	29
Beyond the Edge of Cloud	30
Butterfly Snap	31
Enmity	32
Dingo	33
Hunter	34
Watching Light	36
Cockatoos	37
Raptor	38
Time Freeze	39
For Elma Roach	40
The Lonely Graves	42

The Jumbling of Love	44
Sky Rocket	46
Wait	47
The Colour of Rage	48
Defiance	49
Bounced	50
All Locked Up	51
All in the timing	52
Noted	53
Rules of Engagement for Football and War	54
The Lake	55
Note to Joel	56
Handmade	57
Pole School Blues	58
Letter to Younger Self	59
Father, 2012	60
Splinter	61
Rewind	62
Mum	64
Threads	66
Hush	69
It's All In the Song	70
Finding Me	71
One Child's Winter	72
Winter With Hughie	74
Second-hand	76
Naming Love	77
Changeling	78
Finding Louisa	80

The Forming of Birds

Colours weave through the malleable air of the afternoon, the crowd
shifts, forms and reforms, stepping on the soft green underfoot, cloud-wisped
blue above, the song of little ones chattering, laughing, calling out as
they dance across the space. Here they sit, small arms stretching up
from low chairs, brows knitted intense in concentration, tiny hands busy
with the forming of the firm, damp clay; figures emerge, the clay slowly
pushed, pulled, prodded, stretched, kneaded, scored and marked; the birds
sit, silent but poised, ready to take flight in the imagination of children.

Hand-knitting Peace

Shape-shifting *Dungala* craypots swing languid in the warm afternoon, heavy with wool, with ribbon, with tangle of poetry and stories.
The people walk past, slow, stop – smiles emerge across faces as strands are picked up, messages scribbled on banderole, wool and cloth lengths hand-knitted through the old river-swept string, small children hunkering underneath to weave from within, a gaggle of little girls stops and one affixes a small plastic handbag – she stands back, smiles, satisfied, and moves on, and the mood of love swathes the rusted iron gates that span the space. Embracing, vibrant, abundant with wonderment and the slowing of pace – peace is as one, in the moment; in the now.

Rainbow Harmony

Harmony converges in a riot of colour and noise, fingers threading
softly coloured wool through resting cray pots, stories weaved
in and out of old knots and weathered string, stretching, plucking,
laying down new memories, linking fragments of *Dungala* and cray,
coarse sand and the clacking of river birds, with the lilt of children
chattering across the day; there is a kind of grace in the air, soothing
harshness of message keening across *Te Tai-o-Rehua* – a nascent building
of unbreakable bonds that will not be unravelled by hate and heartache;
we travel accordant, now, our lives looped through and over and together –
like the rainbow we have forged, swinging gently in the afternoon breeze.

Dungala is the Yorta Yorta name for the Murray River.
Te Tai-o-Rehua is the Maori name for the Tasman Sea.

Transformed

The evening sun deepens on the golds and reds and yellows of the
threads and ribbons and narrow strips of cloth as they hang in
rest from the strings of the *Dungala* cray pots, repurposed with love –

the sounds of the day linger in song and *language* and far-off tongue as the
evocative odour of the food vans drifts over the space, rich scents awakening the
longing for tastes, each dish lovingly prepared from culture and hearth

the day has won, as age and religion, country and gender, belief and wonder
are pulled into the vortex of the art, of the moment, as one gesture initiates
the next, and the next until we rest; and are left only with peace and the still life
of interwoven love and sharing hanging gently on the afternoon

Serpent's Tale

Colours shimmer in the gliding –
mountains moving,
making tides.
Legends etched in clapping sticks
tapping stories
in a language fractured
by the conquering.
Riches not of gold
dust-dry scattering
on the burning wind.

Story

Bunggula, the Sooty Grunter (bream), grunts when taken out of the water
> *the duty of Language no longer deserved, reduced to*
> *guttural utterance*

The spines on its back are spears flung by the old man, Baiame, who hunted him
> *to an actor change, the theme remains the same yet*
> *the truth wavers*

in the waterhole. The fish escaped, and as he flashed his tail he made a channel
> *and so always the connection with This Land and*
> *genesis and the ghosts*

which filled with water to make a river / *to caress and slake the thirst,*
> *the stories hang deep and enduring, sung on*
> *by each generation*

But the country dried out, the kangaroos went away, the plants died and there was
> *angry clouds massed, impotent, grumbling revenge*
> *for the desecration caused*

a big drought. The old man came back with his dogs and his sons, and said
> *many truths in song and clapping stick and*
> *white ochre on rock yet*

the drought was because the people didn't know the law or the names of the rivers
> *invasion names drowning out the river voices*
> *bubbling in Language*

He told them the songs to sing and the dances to dance
so the rain would fall again
> *and only some listened and reconciled with*
> *apology and sorrow*

and things would be as they are today
> *as the dead fish pile on putrid river sand and ignorant*
> *greed clogs our arteries*

I acknowledge the use of a Creation story – the story of Baiame and Bunggala the Sooty Grunter – as the inspiration for this poem. I respectfully acknowledge the guardians – and the original storytellers – of the ancestral lands of the Ngemba peoples, and all other affiliated Indigenous peoples, as guardians of the Creation stories and understand the importance of 60,000+ years of continuous connection to and caring for the lands, and respect the tens of thousands of generation who have passed these stories down through storytelling and teaching. The poem was used as an ekphrastic process of stories producing art. The verses and lines in italics are mine.

Corey

We release the balloons
      in dead silence
and they float straight off
no hesitation
no looking back
      there's someone waiting to play with them and
they can't wait to get there.

Way, way up, Bunjil
drops in
checking to see who's flown this high
          this time
recognises the spirit
   dips a prehistoric wing,
      and wheels steeply away

   summoned back into the haze…
      the eagle is suddenly gone.

*

He is six and will not be turning seven
lies so still in the bright, blue box
favourite toy at his chest – a big brave lion…
   and we
cry
   to the tune
    of the Velveteen Rabbit
     and Christopher Robin

try
> to come to terms with listening to
> his high, little voice
> singing from Aunty's phone
his voice
> which will never suffer that cracked warble of
> adolescence before deepening to that of his father.

our sadness tangles in the soft breeze as hearts break
echoing his too-young parents   we gently let go

His journey has begun
drawn forward by dreamtime echoes
sighing gently in ancient tongue
repeating whispers a million years old…

The balloons are out of sight now
yet still we watch   silent…
left with only the memory
of their vibrant colours.

Bunyip

It hunkers in dusked shadows, slowly
flexing and contracting with each laboured
breath, growing ever larger – curved
tusks glistening under glower of eye

Kaieltheban woman drifts in lee of current
feet sculpt digging tool, scrunching coarse
river sand through arch and heel, scoops up
hard-shelled mussel, clammed fearful and closed

her story ripples over gill and scale, dips
through billabong, climbs clay bank on
lizard toe and lifts into hot cicada'd air,
is picked up by the river birds clacking
gossip passed on from beak to bone
to clawed perch view in eucalypt canopy
where expectant…they watch

she senses a shift, feels the warp and weft
of her songline being tugged and snapped,
raw and savage the air bridles and writhes
rends open with teratoid roar, and
she is suddenly gone – removed from
Language from this moment forward…

but now, the river birds sweep up the
wail, screech it from outpost to outpost
squall raucous narrative along Kaiela, snaking
through time, away and away
they refine the refrain, perfect
the chorus, lay down the coda of loss…

they know this song, they have heard it before.

Body Singing

my skin feels his presence
before I know he is there

lithe and silent, he glides
from the back room, appears

in skin that carries songlines
of wind and dust and blood

moves like dance, with feet
that whisper of *bigarrumdja*

displaces the air around me
with his breath, invisible

palpable, and the sigh of story
anchored inexorably to time

a frisson shudders through
all I have known, I stand

mute, unable to answer
the unspoken accusation

as shadow of bone pricks
pointing cold and pale.

bigarrumdja – Yorta Yorta language word for emu

Singing With Both Hands

he punctuates the
wash of schoolyard sound
with the firm, rapid strokes
of confident hands
traces his story
permanent as voice
precise as dance
on each precious minute

a ballet of shadows bounces softly
off red-brick walls
in place of Baghdad echoes
but out playing soccer
he blends seamless, adept
where all are fluent
in one, swift language.

Boat Talk

strange syntax
hard to hold
in the mouth
rolls hesitant
over refuged tongue,
spills out into sanctuary of
the Goulburn river flats
languidly throwing
mirror image of cicada'd gum

a heartbeat away
Christmas Island
holds court in
Flying Fish Cove
sweeps protest swiftly
under righteous surf –
stories stilled
one breath from asylum

and we pause in our day
to witness the truths so
carefully framed
in the 6 o'clock news

Amal's Voice

Listen! She commands; this is the reason she breathed
air not water, the reason she was spared; Listen!

They had drifted, boatless now, hope dissolving
on cold waves, and she watched – helpless – as they

ate the water in their frenzied flight; talks desperately
of crowning baby, cord-joined to wave-gagged mother

and as they swallowed silence, last tears brimmed
oceans that swam to distant shores, tagged land's edge

and lapped gracefully back to salty womb,
to relentless ebb and flow, to and fro. And

so it comes to bear that, on another crabbed
beach, a boy lies as sleeping, curled against the

sand, his dreams of freedom float gently nearby
in lapping wavelets; and then, the sea is no longer

angry – it has had its quota, today, of souls
has swallowed them as they swallowed it.

Amal's voice talks urgently to the Storyteller and
he weaves her tales into beautiful, sad words

like winged secrets escaping Pandora's box, Amal's
voice can be ignored, denied; but never silenced.

Now, she has been called and at last, she too can
sleep, amid the chatter of love and the clatter of

life. Her job is done and she has joined the
story and those who sleep in the ocean, now

her voice lies on white pages, is sung in poetry,
swoops over oceans and deserts, cleaves to memory…

Amal's voice keens softly, insistently, lovingly;
and after she has died, the birds, they keep singing.

This poem was inspired by Arnold Zable's 'The Ancient Mariner', a story about Amal Basry, published in his book *Violin Lessons*.

Aleppo

Spun-gold angels swaddled in pure anguish
spear hearts a million miles away yet distant
tears cannot wash the stain off humanity's
soul – we hold our breath and wait for a deliverance
that never comes.

Syria

The good lady Asma smiles in Instagrammed
style, gracious in studied elegance, while voiceless
babies, spun from the very gold, breathe torturous air
and poisonous decrees from her visionless fool

Yet Still We War

She sits quite still, holds his hand now
her soft touch traces the pink-shell
crescents adorning the end of
delicate fingers,
plays monkey grip with his ticklish fist

she thinks how this hand skips tiny pebbles
through the dust, against the bricks, hears
his giggle as they bounce off, splay in all directions
holds this memory, like a captured
still in a home-movie, grainy and flickering
holds her breath to suspend the moment

he greets each new day as an adventure
smiles as she dishes up breakfast, has not
yet learned who he is or where he belongs, just
is – in the moment – of the moment – touching,
exploring, each new discovery
grasped with tiny, chubby fists of glee.

The day has receded, she does not
register the spit of rain, cannot separate
it from the hiss of rocket, thrum of
drone, it all begins to roll into one, a
whining of hate and radicalised fervour
and the crumbling of stone, imploding

the rubble has settled, with resigned
sigh and dust-breath, and she leans in,
her body jams hard against what is left of the
house. She sits quite still, holding fast
now, traces a delicate vein as far as she
can until it is swallowed by the mass, grasps
his tiny hand, is drawn inexorably
into the darkness.

The Drowning of Angels

Up there – the wind sings through sharp
teeth, shreds entreaties and prayers

and the crumbling dreams that drift on
chilled waves one breath from asylum.

Down here – they of the land are without
voice or account. Limbs respond elegant

to moon's push and pull, dance graceful
on currents until undertow tugs,

draws them deep into *haliae* worlds
down to where the light is squeezed

where sand-bedded seaweed waves
and trails in mockery of wind-filled forests.

Down here, there is an order to things
that scorns all doctrine and prophets

and angels who cannot swim. Instead,
fish feed on breathless skin, beauty and

souls stripped in crabbed feast by tiny,
cold crustaceous teeth. Here, time no

longer matters, is indifferent to the stretching
sorrows, absorbs the grieving of mouths

forever silenced by the shipwreck of broken
boats and a humanity that has turned its back.

Unravelling

He was crinkly at the corners and curves
like someone had unpicked his knit, hand-rolled
the wool and stitched him all over again with
the kinks in different places to his angles

a patina of grime-etched timelines cob-webbed across
the hoary surface of his face – an inexorably keening poem
in staggered, fractured stanzas, attended by rattling
fingers throwing silent shadows to secretive places;

we passed at one of those split-second, unplanned,
blink-and-you-miss moments and I heard his breath
suck in as he squeezed his presence smaller, lesson hard-
learned on crazy streets where shrinking your self saves you…

I stretched out in middle-class empathy, all care and intent
but the moment splintered; his unspent words – hoarded
and shined – cleaved the air, pattering silently to an
indifferent ground. He shuffled away   into crumbling echo
snagged fragments of his discordant life unravelling into the night.

The Leaving of Angels

Who knows first where evil's seeds are sowed
Thrust deep sharp blade of vicious pain
Two *angels* fade away in Millers Road

And there where once their vibrance glowed
Bearing crazy wounds, two lie slain
Who knows first where evil's seeds are sowed

Beyond them now their pooled blood flowed
Night/day alone together are lain
Two *angels* fade away in Millers Road

As grief finds special signs unload
Life's normal ways we do now feign
Who knows first where evil's seeds are sowed

All's left is tears, to lost ones ode
Reason's gone for all, no win, no gain
Two *angels* fade away in Millers Road

Together we shoulder torturous load
Ever caught adrift in sadness' rain
Who knows first where evil's seeds are sowed
Heaven calls two *angels* home from Millers Road

Arranging the Day

for Colleen

I unfold myself into the dawn
stretch to fill the space
wonder how you would have arranged things
with your photographer eye

I follow the sun as it drags the day behind it
trailing scraps of cloud and ragged memories
each, beating second a relentless replacement
cancelling all that has gone before

Later, a slur of movement smears a
crimson finger-painting across the dusk
a subtle rub of colour against the evanescence
committing to another tomorrow, without you.

Beyond the Edge of Cloud

parched paddocks
have thrown up their stalks in despair
have retreated under a layer of dusky silk
which muffles the anguish of
heavy-stepping Blundstones
striding out the measure of failure
tempered yet   by disbelief

in town, the odd verdant lawn
flaunts   look at me!
whilst unnourished front-yard dustbowls
are suddenly politically correct
and the only hint of rain is
the tantalising mirage
stretching ad infinitum
out along the highway

at the local abattoir
pens are crammed to bursting
with unwanted lambs
and the letting of blood
flows from the kill floor
in a grotesque shadow play
of a parallel universe
where all the rivers run

Butterfly Snap

It just takes a split second for life to change
one minute you are fluttering along, minding
your own business and next thing a whacking great
willy wagtail has taken your body, just bloody-well
snapped you up, in mid-bloody-flight if you please

and it's not like you are an endangered species
or anything, just your garden variety Vanessa kershawi
so no special protection expected – except for a little
bit of respect for a fellow-winged creature. Such
a strange sensation, the separation of wing from self and

I do remember feeling somewhat…disembodied, as if
I had transcended myself until I realised this is a bit beyond
your mere common butterfly, yet I did experience a fleeting
moment of pure poetry in motion, and a kind of
weightlessness until I realised that this was due to my

wings wandering off in a frolic of their own, a quavering
semibreve of tissue-thin membrane weighted X10000 with
coloured scales and hairs of forewing and hindwing, out
of synch with the figure-8 synchronicity of wing-beat,
now – post-wagtail – fluttering gently to earth without me

and I felt a gentle fade-out, a darkening of the day and it
seems that time has wrinkled, has stuttered and spluttered
and I sense a slowing of seconds and I try to rewind the
moment, to reverse the second of time but too late –
a single swoop/snap has changed my trajectory and…

Enmity

I bleach
on clay bank,
ssseep sun's warmth
through layered ssscale
gleaming in new birth
the rigour of belly dirt-dancing
has shed the sin, crusted
layers rubbed clean on
rough truths and old taunts. I carry
your bruise, stamped indelible and
ancient as I weave patterns on
shadow, the earth whispering
secrets as it glides away beneath
my story; I've shed my
legs, my ears, my eyelids
no need for approval nor
permissions, I spoke truth
and rent the garden
asunder – your heel seeks to
crush yet I endure, continue,
ever-restless, over country
and time, weaving truth
into the fabric of each
reaching moment that new
morning greets. Imagine me then
sliding through your darkest minutes
wraith-shifting through
your desperate bulwark,
holding, biding
coiling in cold
wait.

Dingo

We had stopped the car at 1400 metres, climbed out and
wandered along the climbing path, taking photos and
wondering gently about the lives of those buried in those
abandoned graves, then…we saw him – seeing us

He trotted unhurriedly along hidden path, almond-shaped
eyes staring confident and unafraid, then he stopped and
…sat…
and we changed direction and headed toward the car and I
felt a fear stretch from within back thousands of years

primal fear, imprinted invisible and hidden
suddenly grabs my throat, pounds my chest
turns my legs to something resembling untamed
fluid and I hurry, hurry, hurry to safety as the
fear tasers into my flesh, stretches back into time
and things I cannot know, yet do, somehow do
and he watches, this assassin, this alpine dingo
this descendant of yesterday's world and suddenly
millennia have kaleidoscoped and I cannot breathe.

He watches. Still and silent. He is wolf.

Hunter

night sly
red-brown fur furrowed by
the quickening breeze
you step noiselessly across
dew-speckled blades
which part silently   then
spring back into shape
in slow-motion replay
as you stalk

your quarry
licks the moisture
from early morning grass
nose quivering,
laden with upwind scents

does not hear you creep
        see your outline on the horizon
                feel your careful consideration
              smell death closing in

Your form leaps high   twists wildly in the gloom
a mad dance in the pre-dawn not-quite light
rabbits scatter
the earth swallowing flashes of white-brown fur
then...

utter stillness
a snarl pushing through the blood on your tapered nose
your stare frozen.

The odour of gunpowder drifts over still air
and I break open the .410,
my fingers burning a little on
the brass head of the shell
as I remove and pocket it,
slide in another,
        sense a flicker of movement
across the morning…

Watching Light

A wave of ibis scribbles wisdom on
curve of morning sky, sweeps high
across cockatoo-confettied eucalypt,
peeling open a crisp autumn day.

I remember this, much later,
watching a Bali sun rise in the same
sky, cicadas chirping sweet and resolute
their song rising on the cloying scent
of hibiscus lifting into humid morning.

I sit, opening your email, to the cacophony
of Bahasa frogs duelling with rice paddy crickets,
arguing the point. I close my eyes and
sense the light spill across the emerging day.

Cockatoos

They paint a moving splash of white and camouflage on the rising sky, a loose line of screeching glee splattering themselves on the fleeting moment and driving wind, screaming across my day as I drive the blue-metal road and I try to keep them in sight and stay on the road at the same time and my gaze switches between road and sky, gets shorter and quicker and I strain to keep them in view even as cruise control rushes me forward and now I throw instant glances at sky-road-verge-ahead-sky-road… and just like that – they are gone and I am gone and the moment in all its glorious, ephemeral purity…is gone.

Raptor

you discard me
as a falconer is
thrown off
by the hawk,
the assassin
artfully arranged
in downy guise

time stretches,
snaps
leaves me
slipstream-gasping
at the swiftness
of your
exodus
your ice-cold perfidy

my bloodied lure
circles madly
through useless air
shrieking anguish
of wingbeat
of a love
as endlessly cursed
as Echo

Time Freeze

Alison Hargreaves, K2, August 1995

You climbed my mountains,
like you I longed to fly –
but I slipped on the ice,
slid back to my quiet despair,
to the warmth of my latitude –
your altitude eludes me.

But it's over now,
like the setting sun
dipping the horizon
you slipped too,
on the edge of reason.
It's there you'll stay –
lore demands –
forever suspended in our minds,
camera lens recording
memories wreathed
in the mists
we weave around heroes.

For Elma Roach

Arranged to advantage
rich fruit poses, languid
secure in impact   smug
cupped by chaste earthenware
and nurturing folds

it takes concentration and time
to catch your lively presence
at fruit's feet –
you compete with
    the flash
        and dash
of exotic
as it splays seductive
seeds and flesh and skin
and spills boldly into our vision –
you sit quietly
beneath
fruit's glory, reflected
soft palette tucked
neatly into place
as required…

yet you are there
patiently awaiting discovery
you *are* there
with tentative jostle
for exposure
a gentle wash of
pink and crimson,
tiered green smudges
announcing
steadfast intention
you are there

if we look

if we see...

The Lonely Graves

She lies, the tiny one, in a small plot
with low narrow wrought-iron fence and
a weathered marble headstone,

the graves up here sparse and scattered
with concrete coverlets, cracked and mossed
home for the lichen that clings tight in

the cold, and I wonder would there still have been
snow, on that October day, on this mountain where
little Bertha died, or had early spring winds begun

softening the frozen white skin that clothed
this high plain – where gold had built a town
that lived only a fleeting existence; had her

father taken to the crisp, hard ground with
pick and shovel as Bertha surrendered into
death only days after struggling into life, did

the tears chill on his face as he prepared an
unforgiving ground to receive his lovingly
swaddled baby, buried a piece of himself.

Now there is nothing but resilient grass crinkled
across this plain adorned with wombat holes
and rabbits and ragged herds of wild brumby

and with these few graves – one close by Bertha,
perhaps to keep her company – the others
separated by gaps that could be nothing yet

may be others more forgotten and rotted
like the tiny space surrounded by rails, no
coverlet here, no name immortalised in stone.

The gold is long gone, taking everything with it
and all that is left is a sparse, desolate graveyard vigil'd
by the lonely, windswept howl of alpine dingo.

The Jumbling of Love

She stretches long, strong arms over her head,
soft blonde shimmer of hair snakes down supple
back as elegant, tanned limbs move sensuously
in the morning sun. She smiles, even white teeth
nestle strongly, just behind soft pillow of lip.
She waits, today, he comes, today, her love, her
boy; her everything.

He will stride around the corner soon, as he
does most days, bound across the front lawn
and leap up to land on the balcony where
she sits waiting. They will wind young
limbs around each other, entwine in breathless
tangle of joy and he will trace lean, strong fingers
down her arm, over her hand, down her back.
He will touch those places that make her tremble
and she will scrape coloured nails lightly down
his back. Their love is a game and it keeps her
grounded. She does not want to think of not
having him. Their love stretches out before them,
a path of diamonds, unfolding into the future.

There is a creak at the gate; she raises her
eyes. Here he comes, walking toward her. The
sun is in her eyes now, she lifts a slow hand
to try and shield her face and the light falls
harshly on the thin skin, mottled and dotted like
a pitted, rotting apple. He walks slowly across
the lawn, the wheels of his walker sinking into
the grass leaving thin twin lines from the gate
to her veranda. He takes one hand in his, places
another on her back and gently rubs between
her shoulders. Hello old girl, he says softly, a tiny
catch in his voice as he watches her struggle to
know him. Nice day, love, he says, kisses her
forehead with his paper-thin lips. She politely
lets him hold her hand. Whoever he is. She smiles
and turns back to the pathway.
Waits,
for her love.

Sky Rocket

There is a rocket in the sky, tonight,
arched against the dark, lit by lunar breath –
the moon, she breathes, silently exhales;
the sky is not black, never black
but blue-grey, a shade cooler than Monday
lightly bruised, smeared with cloud and barbed star –
it is a cloud rocket, cirrus-soft, billowing softly,
folding and stretching, fading inexorably
into pricked fabric of deepening night

Wait

this hour holds its breath
suspended
in the deep-mauve
of a perfect Thursday
aching for rain

The Colour of Rage

Poetry by synaesthesia

I don't have a day to describe
my rage; Mondays are the blue

of bruises, the smudge of sadness
whilst Tuesdays sigh resignedly pale

thin mauve seconds rippling softly
into strong purple Wednesdays

striding deliberately into mid-week
elbowing previous minutes aside whilst

Thursdays slide back into deeper
mauve, blanket the senses with soft

purple smother. Fridays are red-brown
feel soft and warm, bleed into

white Saturdays, stark sharp, slap
into sombre, dark-brown Sunday.

There is no day to describe my rage
red, red hot – I have no day to wear it.

Defiance

Cobwebs string lazily from the fixtures, dust
has settled itself on everything
that does not move and some things that
listlessly do, like the fan that turns in
slightly crooked circles, thudding gently in
uneven hang, marking time in the weight
of the afternoon. The house sighs heavily,
creaks in protests at the shifting it must do as
it settles into the heat. She sits in the detritus of
the family's wake and tells herself the housework
won't do itself. Where to start? So much to
get through. She takes a deep breath, picks up
a pen and begins to write instead. Today,
she will defy the rules. Will fail in her duties.
Instead, today will be the day for poetry and song
and little notes of love.

Bounced

He sways out
of nightclub hubris,
slides a hand along
bricks that slap
vacant shadows back
on a face,
pale with bourbon overload
bruises deepening
to the dull-blue
thumping
of the looming Monday morning.

All Locked Up

This poem was inspired by Sylvia Plath's 'Edge'

A weariness has folded
itself into her form

moulded the future in
statue'd stillness

her likeness chronicled
on implacable morrow as

owl's screech scratches at
scar-bleached night.

Ananke shimmers at cosmos
edge, beckoning as the

universe stutters & signals time
she is thirty and tired

waits patient for indifferent moon
gliding through new phase

to turn her back and
signal final curtain.

All in the timing

I don't know where that moment
went. I had been prepared, waiting

for it, had cleared my diary of tasks
around the time it was done, made

sure I wasn't on the phone, or
locked in Facebook discussion

turned down the telly and started the
coffee machine, lit a lavender melt

I almost had it right, the mood
just then, for that moment, then

you spoke. Your words pattered
around my feet, peppered my

concentration, wrenched me from
my carefully constructed path, so

painfully moulded. The moment
shredded, fluttered softly to

the floor, slithered out the
door, sighing in your wake.

Noted

If I could put notes
in an orderly, melodic line
to the words that
tumble from my fingertips
I'd write you a song…

But instead I can only offer
pieces of me
pulled randomly from
heightened senses
and a world suddenly
upside-down.

Rules of Engagement for Football and War

Old truths hang silent over sweet, sweet grass
Southern Cross sirens bellow battle call
Young limbs entangle, test boundaries far
Slam into the fray as mothers let go

Southern Cross sirens bellow battle call
New boots lay fleeting shadows long
Slam into the fray as mothers let go
Hard-earn the badge of battle-scar

New boots lay fleeting shadows long
Slash new paths on ancient roads
Hard earn the badge of battle scar
And learn too late they travel too far

Slash new paths on ancient roads
Wrench aching songs from jagged throats
And learn too late they travel too far
Whilst old truths hang silent over sweet, sweet grass.

The Lake

I'm all angles, in '69
and knees
conforming to structured games
in a cavernous timber space
that seemed old even then
on the fist of land
that cupped her grey waves
in the middle of
nowhere
a place that sang silently
in a language I was yet to learn

now I pass her
periodically, on my way
to somewhere else
as I will again
this Eel Festival
and as always
she siren-calls
to savour her air
breathe the cold, thin wind
that marks her surface
wear her satin-chill caress
on my bare skin
one day I'll be back
just for her.

Note to Joel

it's almost finished, nearly dead now
that place that kept your mum so busy
no more lunchtime crush
for ham and tomato sandwiches
there's still some of them left
but the wind is beginning to blow
cold and desolate through the gaps
where once they lined up
grabbing the fruit with the rot spots,
sorting on the cross-belts
laughing and bickering and changing
lives melding, shifting, re-sorted
like everything
it's all gone to Shepparton
'cause we know they steal everything!
…hospital, council, cannery…
what's left in Mooroopna is soul, and heart and
a slow, deep feeling
of belonging
and of being left behind.

Handmade

I wander through your art, breathe gently into your vision,
follow the strong brushstrokes through the swoops and swirls
and back-brush, tumble through the interrupted sweep of
commitment, stumble the faint trail of your intent reaching for
the inexplicable,
the untouchable…
and then I see it. It is in the bones of a ship beaching
on ancient, secret shores, of the slashed sails and battered
timbers – our shipwreck, truths that slip slyly through workaday
hands and anguished fingers, of the search for the thing you
cannot name, that which eludes you in
your effort to explain.

Your hands. Hold the camera in such stillness that time itself
is stamped, indelible, unarguable, on the moment. Curved
around the lens in such a manner that truth cannot resist,
holds steady and true and records that which you command.
The tilt and light and angle of vision imprisons the moment
in perfect repose. The brush, though, resists your efforts,
challenges your vision, spits in the eye of your intent.
The camera holds the real, but I live and breathe for the
uncertainty, the doubt, the vulnerability of your art.

Handmade.

Pole School Blues

I grasp the cold metal
feel the strength of it –
straight as nymph's back
smooth as youth's shining skin –
and my body wears the drag, the
dead-weight of age and time
that has silently crept
around my core and there is
nothing sensuous that follows.
Later, I watch the blue-eyed honeyeater
balance his round body on twigged legs
dipping and bobbing gracefully as he
works his way around the banksia,
clawed toes clutching slender
branches at crazy angles, plunging
his rapier beak deep into flower,
a silent ballet orchestrated by the
lure of nectar and a perfect
sense of gravity and self.

I unfold stiffly, into the morning
and wish that I could fly.

Letter to Younger Self

Dear Me,
which could be a salutation or a lamentation, I had so much
to tell you but again we have run out of time and it has been
a hectic day and again we are three steps behind the
impossible schedule I put together for us this week and
already it is nearly Friday and life is slipping through our
fingers and it's all getting so hard to keep up, especially
as we are now a Grandma and there is so much I should
tell you, like believe in yourself and don't sweat the small
stuff and bugger other people's opinions 'cause they really
don't count but if I only warn you about one thing
for our future it is this; keep shaving our legs...
we've taken up pole dancing.

Father, 2012

'When a knife is used to make [cuts] across the grain [(of] wood, the fibres left between the cuts are very short and crumble away as the cuts are deepened.'*

I watch his mind tremble
thoughts tumble from mumbled lips
and I wonder where he is
right now, in his head,
in this room that is   home

back then, his legs strode paddocks
strong hands strung fences
sawed the posts and planks
he moulded with precision
jigsaw pieces snug-fit neat

now, quavering hands fumble
do not recognise touch
of smoothed or rough
the fibre of linking
brain and eye and hand
has crumbled

I read softly to him
from the book of handsaws
kept as carefully as his tools;
eyes closed, he breathes quietly
sawdust memory consumed

* *Concerning Handsaws. Some Hints On Their Care & Maintenance* – Spear & Jackson, published at one shilling

Splinter

We sit suspended in the lull of late afternoon and I hold
his hand. I have trimmed the nails and buffed the edges
smooth, anything to fill the stretching quiescence

His mind sputters and coughs like the misfiring 186 I helped
him to fix all those years ago, when the silence
was all about concentrating on the task

I try to follow as he roils through twilight corridors,
memories flickering like the shaky 8-mil movies with
which he meticulously chronicled our lives

Now it seems he has rambled off-course, his being
has diverged from the essence of him, has peeled slowly
away in a fractured parody of body and soul

He is enigma now, a maze of blood and skin and bone
melded in slow waltz with fragmented memories whispering
slyly in foreign tongue. I touch but cannot reach him.

Rewind

I straighten the photo – you are maybe ten or eleven –
four dogs adore at your feet, all visibly straining to
sit closest to you, resting on the rockery created
by your grandmother, covered in violet-flowered vine.
It is 1938.
I dreamed of you last night and again it was not how you
were when you left us, your mind lost in hazy corridors,
splintered and melded in slow waltz with fragmented
memories whispering slyly in foreign tongue;
it was before…
when you would enthral grandchildren with your stories,
charm all the customers in the supermarket where
you worked, when I could call and you would rescue me
by changing a flat tyre or towing me home when I ran out
of petrol. Again. Winding further back when I railed and
fought at your rules that kept me safe, your values that I
then felt as archaic and strangling, that I then applied to
my own children, back further to all those times you drove
me to swimming and Brownies and all the other things
I felt imperative to my fitting in, back further to when
I sat on the wheel arch of the tractor, rain freezing on my
nose and face as I shadowed your every move, even
down to the limp. The one you acquired at fourteen,
knocked from your bicycle by a dog and carried to hospital
on horseback where you lay for months in traction that
was ill-advised and left you crooked, and you could not
ride that pony at the country show any more. I have that
photo too, and those spurs you wore sit now on a shelf
with your cameras – the Kodak Folding Brownie and the
Bolex 8-mil. Now the memories have folded into time

before me; back to when you and your adored collected
me from the Babies Home and decided it such a good idea
you did it twice again and made one of your own in between;
and before that the gorgeous, jerky, imperfect perfection
of you and Mum in those 8-mil movies, I have never seen
anyone so happy as you two on your wedding day, those
fragile films carefully evacuated from disintegrating
celluloid, transferred to disc then stick, then cloud…and
that is where you are now – in cloud. In memory.
And in my fragmented dreams that ignore your fragility
and deny your slide into an unbalance of self. When I sleep,
those 8-mil movies flicker in time suspended and I dream
of the best you.

Mum

she was waiting for the moon
for the pull and push of lunar lines
turning in rhythm, exact timing
just like when she played

I sit at her piano, touch my fingers
lightly over pitted keys, the echo
of her songs vibrate gently on the air
and I can hear her joyous singing all again

she has slept today, after a restless waking
and her dreams are melding, folding in on themselves
she is confused at whom she sees now
soon it will be at who she is

the sleeping is drawing longer, each day,
with less awake and more at rest
apart from the odd frown and soft murmur
and lately calling out 'Daddy…'

the night is clear and her moon moves silent
across an empty sky; her future here too is
empty, her Darling waits at night's edge
beckoning her forward
sighing soft love letters, one by one

she hovers gently in between now
hearing her beloved's call,
murmurs spasmodically in
code as her mind wanders unknown corridors

it is almost time; soon she will shed
her Self and move smoothly
into the light. Her beloved waits for her,
perhaps a smile and outstretched hand,
beckoning her forward with Heaven's promise
and vows unbroken.

Threads

Amongst the refined clatter of
early morning breakfast
and civilised footsteps on
smart, wooden floors under
stylish exposed brickwork and
thick wooden beams,

Cate reads to us
of the old bull

and I find myself back in the yard at Kolora
with its drystone walls and cobblestones
thin, thin winds and the biting rain
slicing at a face that cowers
under a thick, woollen hat
worn with red corduroy overalls
and a colourful woollen pullover
hand-knitted with love

        and I hear the sound of him once more.

I visit my father
who does not read poetry
who has no ear for music yet accompanies Mum
to Foster and Allen and
Soup and Song,
and he laughs and nods as we

try to remember his name,
the old fool,
Ben, says Mum, but no
that was the young bull
until finally Dad remembers,
his face showing relief,
Frankliffe Advancer
he says firmly and we laugh and remember with him

I read it to my husband,
the television on mute
he has half an ear for me
and both eyes on the TV – Jack Palance is back on after
the ads – I finish in a hurry as he motions for the remote

I wave back at him
– only three more lines
listen, can't you, this is good!

what do you think? I ask
yeah, well, she knows what she's talkin' about
he drawls
butcher, slaughterman, cow farmer's son
as if knowing your stuff is
more important than the poetry

I contemplate reading it to my son
when he returns
from dogging, outback,
and though it may seem
he should understand
I fear the memory is too thin
to be stretched this far
something will be lost
in the thread of time
in the knowing of this story

He will gaze at me
as only a teenage son can do with
barely disguised disinterest and say
yeah, that's good, Mum
and turn away
leaving me only with a faint echo of
my father's invincibility,
rain freezing on my nose and cheeks
and Frankliffe's anguished bellowing
resounding across an empty paddock.

Hush

I shackled you
to my bedoom wall
as I lay beneath,
pubescent body on fire,
and I remember how you swung
across the stage
swaying in music-beat
your long, lean torso
fluid,
sinuous
your movements all suggestion
and promise
the sharp crease in your flares
and the thrust of your hips
crackling like lightning strike
and I could almost believe
you were looking at me

tonight, your siren-song begins
and we ride the wave,
again,
for one brief moment
until   the lights go up,
and I blink
walk out into the cool night
secretly hug you to me
one last time.

It's All In the Song

It's getting dark; the sky is lined with rumbling grey clouds tumbling
into the approaching night. A lone cricket has taken up the challenge
in close whilst a distant cricket orchestra cymbals gently out further on
the dusk. The dog over the back fence barks, a general who goes there?
type enquiry – a single yelp answered immediately and calmly by my
own dog – and I sense a canine sharing 'what?' 'yeah', 'you OK?' exchange.
The night closes in; a pair of plovers squall, untraceable, across the
arc of dimmed sky, raising distant, primitive fears. The cricket chorus chirps on,
dragging wing-edge over wing-edge, calling loudly now for their girls,
stridulating, boasting, jostling for position in the close summer night air…
his hands push insistently on my shoulders, press my body into the
damp, coarse river sand, his breath hot and sour with rum and cigarettes
hovers, a silencing;
the night stirs and rustles…and the crickets don't miss a beat.

Finding Me

I stand at the angle best seen by my mirror
strain to catch the lean lines of form

but they have been consumed, swallowed
by the rest of my body, swelled to enormous

ambushed, I press myself into the dusk
try to disappear into the dark, but I am bulk.

He touches with light tongue, insistent
flicks his way through the flesh,

skin whispers on skin, tracing slick promise
on a body that cannot remember itself.

I once fitted neat, side-saddle on the bar
of my boy's bicycle, his lithe form

curved protectively at my back, his breath
fluttered hotly, sighing sweet promise

we flew through warm summer night
on strong legs and teenaged eros

now his mouth challenges and I feel
he has coloured outside the lines.

One Child's Winter

the pulse of machines
sucks warm milk
swishes through the cloudy sight-glass
pumps along the pipes and hoses
through the wall
and down the cold, tin ripples
into the vat

she clambers up the steps
stands tiptoe
the tin scoop banging
as she skims the surface
draws the cream

mixes the calf powder
carefully measuring that one bucket makes three
hot, hot water
bursts the bubbles of powder
then eats the mixture
smears sticky across her face
just like the calves
as they snuffle the buckets

the cats
turn up morning
and night
to drink warm milk from old sardine cans
she carries the scrap bucket,
bumps against her short legs,
down to the chook pen
where they mix scoops of layer pallets
into the scraps
and add hot water

can still catch the odour
on days of careful memory
of the crisp morning
her father took her down to meet
the newborn lambs
and her wonderment at the sliver-thin sheen of ice
covering the puddles
she gently probed with woollen-gloved fingers.

Winter With Hughie

the breath of a child
against cold glass
a canvas for fingertip masterpiece
rubbed out with a grimy palm
and childish giggles

and he sits beside her
huffs against the windscreen
traces the elegant, spidery lines
that she held in such awe,
tests her
from the purple spelling book
she has brought home from school
– spell 'hippopotamus', Sweetie, he says –
and admonishes her
when he catches her peeking

    and just who, she wonders
was minding whom
when they sat reading
to the pulse of machines
rhythmically sucking at warm milk,
waiting for her father, his son…

and she wonders – now –
what memories teased at the fear
he swallowed down hard
with each long day
as he sat
trapped into submission on
a hip broken early,
by poverty and grind and a bastard Irish father,
then set hard
by Flanders mud

and she remembers how they sat quietly together
as he traced truth on clouds
patiently teaching her
more than words.

Second-hand

I stretch in every direction these aged sinews and muscles and ligaments allow, suspend unattached and feather-light in the water, lose perspective of time and place and me; contemplate the innocence of the sky above, unmarred by cloud and opinion.
Time stands.
Right now, I have no place; no presence; no niche – I have just the moment, fluid and soft and undulating, looking up at the same sky that she would have looked at…second-hand baby, I scrabble for purchase on my timeline, carefully refine the narrative, each recounting laying down memory and story, fold upon fold of time and point and belonging. At birth I was placed; inserted neatly and conveniently, a planted seed in a well-tended garden; watered, fed, nurtured and trellised. The years undulate through the story and I scramble to sort it into a timeline I can divine.   Placed.   Or displaced.

Naming Love

The name on my first birth certificate does
not fit me; the name on my second echoes
the older brother I never knew; a caress
lovingly bestowed on a changeling; I wear
it in safe harbour, carry the memory
of he who lies in the arms of angels.

My existence hangs on unplanned and
unwanted moments in other people's
lives, yet I do not feel unwanted. I wear
my name in silent, weightless love.

Changeling

'...Parliament expresses our formal and sincere apology to the mothers, fathers, sons and daughters who were profoundly harmed by past adoption practices in Victoria.' – Parliamentary Apology, Government of Victoria, Australia, 2012

My mother never knew my face
no touch of tiny fingers
counted toes or holding close
yet she felt me

insistently, I would have pushed
against soft membrane
fluttered, elbowed and booted
gently swelling against convention

maybe I announced myself with
hiccups and heartburn and a sadness
too empty to describe
if she had been allowed;

the succour of mouth and nipple
denied, how she must have cried
with only imagined imprint of
touch to scar empty palms

the years have now ticked
full lifetimes and yet
the mirror traps echoes,
each glance a question

A changeling, amorphous and unconnected
our shadows do not touch
I have no measure, nor memory
just these hands that I watch.

Finding Louisa

Until that year that I knew of my birth father until the
month that I spoke with those aunts until the
hours that we met I had no knowledge nor memory
of Louisa yet I sensed her there suspended
in time the

vulnerability of her station and sex and standing was
complex yet colonially staid and stagnant and her youth
was no protection against men and the whoring aspect of
reality in those days and on the waterfront the
long redgum

port drawing swarms from all over the branches and
leaves holding black against the dimming sky-blue of the
night tinges of gold and streaks of creamy crimson
smears across the moment as it segues and
morphs into

continuous dusk then dim then the night dark night
touching on the insignificant curve of concrete head-stone
cleaving broken pitted and illegible to the sand-clay soil
of the river flats that I swirl through my toes as I trawl
through her short

life babe at breast dead at eighteen so-called father's name
tacked awkwardly after death onto the lowly monument staged
at the back end of the cemetery left to disintegrate into
nothing where they pressed her down they pushed her out of

memory. I found Louisa today and now I will follow the hours to know her more and there is a subtle shift in the

day in the knowing/not knowing as I start all over again adding more layers to the story

of me.

www.ingramcontent.com/pod-product-compliance
Lightning Source LLC
Chambersburg PA
CBHW062148100526
44589CB00014B/1737

9781761091773